*This*
Christmas Memories
*book belongs to:*

Made in China
From CANDLEWICK GIFT. Made exclusively for Borders.
Inspired by the book *Willow at Christmas*. Copyright © 2002 by Camilla Ashforth.
0-7636-2010-6